courrèges

Translated from the French by Lorna Dale

First published in Great Britain in 1998 by Thames and Hudson Ltd, London

Copyright © 1998 by Editions Assouline, Paris

British Library Cataloguing-in-Publication Data
A catalogue record for this book is available from the British Library

ISBN 0-500-01895-2

Printed in Italy

courrèges

Text by Valérie Guillaume

Thames and Hudson

the philosopher Roland Barthes, asked for his views on André Courrèges' success, rekindled the controversy between traditionalists and modernizers. 'You only have to look at Chanel's timeless "chic" to see that women are already wearing (and know how to wear) the "new" look that Courrèges is so determined to create for them' (*Marie Claire*, September 1967). Courrèges is a visionary with his own individual approach to fashion. He prefers to liberate himself from traditional influences and not look to the past for inspiration. This immediate response to modern life has had a tremendous impact, as Yves Saint Laurent has acknowledged. 'I found it difficult to break away from traditional elegance and Courrèges changed that' (Laurence Benaïm, *Yves Saint Laurent*, Paris, 1993, p. 138). Courrèges saw his task as somewhere between a youthful and optimistic inventiveness and a concept of fashion embracing the platonic ideal of perfect form. 'What was needed was to apply new technical and aesthetic rules and create a modern style that was easy to wear.'[1]

When Courrèges set up his own couture house in the autumn of 1961, his first priority was to put the past behind him and 'forget' his work for Balenciaga. 'You had to think the same way as he did. I followed the boss's ideas and Coqueline and I carried them on when we set up our own business. The most difficult part was getting away from them and finding ourselves on our own, with only our own resources to fall back on. It was very hard work. I was so much under Balenciaga's influence and loved his work so much that it was three or four years before I could put it behind me and develop a style of my own. I left Balenciaga in 1960–61 and it took me until 1964 to find my own identity. When you have worked somewhere for ten years, you start doing things automatically. I paid for my admiration and interest with hard work. Coqueline left shortly before I did and she helped me make the move.'

André Courrèges recalls how he virtually forced his way into Balenciaga. 'I saw a couple of his designs and was bowled over. I decided that that was where I wanted to work.' I spoke to Jean Barthet, an old friend from Béarn province, and to Mme Castaynié, who ran *L'Officiel de la couture*. She tried to get an appointment for me, but that was not possible. So then I went to a team of smugglers in Hendaye who carried Balenciaga's patterns and designs. I had a letter passed on to him and I met him.' In fact, he remembers suggesting that he should work for Balenciaga for nothing, 'as a junior apprentice'. Balenciaga took him on in a tailoring atelier. André Courrèges learned the business and progressed rapidly. After five years Balenciaga sent him to his

Eisa couture houses in Spain to give him 'more freedom and responsibility'. When he returned, Courrèges went to Balenciaga and told him, 'Nothing grows under a tall tree. I am a little acorn and you are a great oak. I have to leave you to survive.' It was three years before Balenciaga gave him permission to set up his own couture house. 'I could have left straight away. But when I did, our parting was amicable. One day he came to see me and said, 'Are you leaving? Do you need money? I'll give you some. Do you need help with administration? I'll send you my manager. Do you need clients? I'll send you clients."'

Although he has never courted publicity, Cristobal Balenciaga's dramatic use of materials, colours and shapes is unrivalled. Everything bore his stamp, but he sometimes left it to André Courrèges and another of his close associates, Ramón Esparza, to cater for younger tastes. 'I had to think like him, and I must say that was no problem for me', Courrèges admits. 'Balenciaga taught me about the seventeenth century. The aesthetic simplicity of his clothes and mine was inspired by that period.' It was an interest they had in common, often visiting Spanish antique dealers in search of religious artefacts (Courrèges later restored a seventeenth-century farmhouse in the Basque village of Urrugne). Their common roots, in the Basque country and the Béarn, must have been a bond (Balenciaga was born in Guéthary, Courrèges in Pau and Coqueline in Hendaye). Coqueline also worked for Balenciaga, first in a tailoring and later a dressmaking atelier. She never had access to the studio but says, 'I still saw everything that went on.'

André and Coqueline Courrèges both come from a remote part of rural France and have never lost their regional accents. They brought something of their native soil and history to the most purist of Paris couture houses. As the philosopher Alain so aptly put it in one of his *Propos*, 'Look at the man, the sky and the earth and get his measure straight away.' In the 1950s Balenciaga taught the Courrèges to maintain a strict discipline in their work.

Courrèges always preferred flat shoes. They make women walk in a particular way, from the thigh and hip rather than the leg, moving the whole of the lower limb like a dancer. Coqueline Courrèges recalls how women who until then had been restricted by tight skirts and high heels were suddenly skipping along. 'Women needed to be able to walk and run again. And I was a dancer myself.' Flat heels forced the designer to recalculate the proportions of the female body. This created a delicate balance and a hat was essential 'to fill out the silhouette'. The garment had to fall from the shoulders and was accompanied by a mid-calf sock or boot. 'The clothes float. You don't feel them. I don't emphasize the waistline because the body is a whole. It is ridiculous to treat the top and bottom parts of the body separately.'

It was this straightforward approach that produced the miniskirt. For a long time its origins were controversial. Who actually invented it: Courrèges or Mary Quant, the French or the British? Coqueline Courrèges recalls a trip to London in 1964 when she received a *Sunday Times* prize and appeared in front of an audience from the fashion trade. 'Mary Quant was there. I remember she sold a lot of knitwear in her boutique in the King's Road.' Courrèges was the first to include a mini outfit in one of his shows, in January 1965. Mary Quant soon followed his example, popularizing the shorter skirt during the famous 'swinging sixties' in Britain. Along with the Beatles she received official recognition 'for her contribution to the revival of Britain's cultural influence and for boosting foreign trade' (B. Lemonnier, *L'Angleterre des Beatles, une histoire culturelle des années soixante*, Paris, 1995, pp. 211–12).

The mini completely altered the image of the body. Courrèges' pared-down style with its calculated proportions creates a dynamic silhouette, allied to movement. It has elements of Futurism and Constructivism. Like the avant-garde Russian and German artists of the 1920s and 1930s, Courrèges reveals the internal structure, the machine stitching on the clothes. The top-stitching on the edging or highlighting the seams is like 'the pencil strokes in the preliminary sketch', emphasizing the shape and structure of the garment. This is a new and poetic vision of man's relationship to the world. Courrèges' austerity has its roots in the Bauhaus, the famous German school of art, architecture and design founded in 1919. The proportions of the belt (worn low in the 1960s) or the half-belt are calculated from the shoulder line. 'I made the garment fall away from the body by starting from the shoulders. Darts were no longer necessary.' However, these parallel, vertical and horizontal lines are softened by cutaway armholes, curved scallops or rounded patch pockets (*Elle*, March 1968). Courrèges used thick material like whipcord, a type of gaberdine, and double-sided materials which allowed the seams to be tucked in and top-stitched. The double-sided material is made of two fabrics between which, Coqueline Courrèges says, 'we inserted an interlining to make the gaberdine fuller and rounder.' Each side is in a different material or colour: cotton on top, cotton or a synthetic material underneath, wool in between or plain on one side, patterned on the other (*Marie Claire*, March 1965). 'Courrèges fabric is equally strong on the weft and the warp'. Balancing fairly heavy weights and measurements 'taken with a string, a set square and a compass' (advertisement for the Spring/Summer 1965 show), Courrèges calculates the garment's proportions so as to complement the wearer's movements.

two years later, a Courrèges collection was likened to 'a performance of gymnastics, dance and music' (*L'Officiel de la couture*, September 1967), and in March 1969 the pace was just as exuberant. The crescendo-decrescendo jazz accompaniment to the 1965 Spring/Summer show and the 'jerk' music for the 1967 spring-summer show were something entirely new, according to contemporary witnesses. The energetic movements on the catwalk, inspired by 'happenings' (a type of performance art that became popular in the early 1960s), allowed the models complete freedom of expression. This in itself was a kind of cultural revolution. The relationship between a woman and her body, other people and nature was physical and not sculptural, as it had been in the 1950s. 'The models, often girls we met in the street, have to tell us about what they are wearing. Courrèges made the fashion world recognize and reflect the role of sport in modern life. French couture houses had been making sportswear since the Paris Olympics in 1924, producing special ranges of swimwear, beach outfits, shorts and ski pants alongside their haute couture. But Courrèges was not simply designing yet another range of sportswear. For him sport represented a way of life, a code of behaviour. He was an athlete himself; he played pelota and rugby and enjoyed mountaineering. Coqueline liked dancing. 'André is an expert skier', she said proudly. Their models were always tanned and athletic-looking. In the first issue of *Sportswear International* in January 1971, Courrèges was quoted as saying that for him life was a kind of sports contest. He saw each working day as a sporting challenge. Asked whether he considered himself a sportswear designer, he replied: 'Definitely. I love that look, not only for trousers, jumpsuits and body stockings, but for dresses and coats as well.'

I n the early 1970s Courrèges continued his quest for novelty. He was not trying to create 'classic' fashion on the lines of the Chanel suit or Balenciaga's tunic dress, which perhaps explains why these were the only two twentieth-century designers he admired, describing them designs as 'masters of couture. One was an architect, the other's trademark was femininity'. His ambition was to create a new style of clothing, a metaphor for the fit and athletic body. 'Creation is dreaming up shapes, like the jumpsuit or body stocking, or developing new versions of the trouser suit, which the Chinese discovered a long time before we did' (*Elle*, August 1970). The first jumpsuit, in thick two-tone wool jersey, belted at the hips and with a zip front, was shown in 1967. In 1968 *Elle* published a picture of the 'all-in-one body stocking', a seamless double-rib garment covering the body from neck to toe. 'The stitch is the opposite of warp and weft, which gives volume. The stitch creates a second skin.' *Jardin des Modes* says that the close-fitting garment is for women who are becoming more and more confident about their bodies. The body stocking marks the advent of the 'body-look' (March 1970). In 1971 Courrèges said, 'The second skin is a style of clothing that fits the contours of the body exactly. I think everyone will be wearing it in three to four years' time. It is an irreversible trend, that's the way the world is going' (*Sportswear International*). Costume historians will recognize the garment as a modern version of Dr Rasurel's famous 'healthy' knitted underwear, very popular in the early part of the twentieth century. Comfort is still important and this was not the only example of underwear becoming outerwear.

The original 'second skin body stocking' was worn under a pinafore dress – short, of course, and sleeveless. Later versions were worn with a blouson jacket, in contrasting materials and colours. Of the three men's and seven women's outfits that

Courrèges designed in 1972 for the fifteen thousand staff at the Munich Olympics 'the two most typical' featured the body stocking. 'You can't cheat with a blouson and certainly not with a body stocking, any more than you can cheat in sport' (*Elle*, 28 August 1972).

t he range of colours that Courrèges employs is unique. His use of white is inspired by: white-walled houses; Basque pelota players dressed in white and playing against a white wall; villages in southern Spain where, in Courrèges' words, 'even the streets and pavements are whitewashed and just looking at them makes you feel good' (*Jardin des modes*, March 1975); and by the white of the clothes that Coqueline's father always wore. Coqueline recalls that 'in the Avenue Kléber everything was white, the walls, the chairs, the cushions with the pompons round the edges and the carpet'. The décor in the Rue François-Ier, with its plastic flooring, painted wood, formica, and leather pouffes, was equally monochrome but not so completely mat. The white surroundings created a gleaming and luminous space in which the body moved as though weightless.

In the preparation of fabrics, bleaching is the stage before dyeing. After 'boiling off', which cleans them and removes any impurities, they are bleached to make them white enough for dyeing or printing. A new bleach, optical blueing agent, was introduced in the late 1960s. This produced brilliant white fabrics which displayed a fluorescent bluish-purple tinge when seen in daylight. Courrèges always had a penchant for this 'optical' white. 'We discovered true white when we wanted to introduce colour; we found it impossible to position the shades against the normal black cardboard backing or on the beige of human skin. We wanted a bluish white, which is very difficult to achieve.' At the time, new fibres and materials such as synthetics were being developed and these helped because they 'made the background very easy to bleach'. White and silver were the fashionable colours in the 1960s. This was the 'space age' – in 1961 the Russian cosmonaut Yuri Gagarin made the first ever manned space flight, in 1965 Edward White's weightless excursion into space was shown on television and in 1969 Neil Armstrong became the first man to walk on the moon. In that period white was everywhere, in photography, film, design and interior décor. For Courrèges it was a symbol of cleanliness and purity. 'People wear black because it does not show the dirt. Every morning they put their dirty clothes back on. Nowadays you have to be clean inside and out' (*Radioscopie* by Jacques Chancel, 1973, quoted in *L'Officiel de la couture*, December 1993, p. 38). White shows the dirt and needs regular care, a simple matter with modern washing machines.

●

In Courrèges couture, and in their design and décor, colour creates a spiritual link with the world. Coqueline says that when André was serving in the French Air Force in 1944, 'He saw the Americans landing, dressed in blue and white. Even their flannelette pyjamas were sky-blue. It all made a deep impression on André.' Colour is part of a mystical symbolism that is essentially optimistic, because seeing life through rose-coloured spectacles also creates a good mood. 'My work is made up of colours, structured around white, reflecting the light, azure blue reflecting the cosmos and silver reflecting the moon' (*L'Officiel de la couture*, December 1993).

Not only did the Courrèges find a new kind of white, but they also discovered transparency, evoking sometimes air and sometimes water, or sometimes the sky and sometimes the sea, depending on their creative inspiration. The drawing – the first stage in their designs – superimposes a sketch on paper on one or more transparent sheets of Rhodoïd on which they draw in ink or felt-tip pen. 'We work like printers, using a flat frame. Without Rhodoïd it would be impossible to draw in white on a white background,' says Coqueline. 'In 1962 we also started cutting the Rhodoïd into strips and weaving it with ribbon in cloth weave. Later, when we discovered Swiss guipure from Saint-Gall, we inserted round cut-outs of this transparent material in the holes in the embroidery.'

Courrèges sees his creations as a vehicle for ideas that are not constrained by fashion. His inspiration comes from the modern world of industry and not the world of fashion, which in his opinion is too driven by styles and trends. Like anyone breaking new ground he is often thought of as 'crazy'. Courrèges uses man-made materials for town wear, because 'with town wear people are not innovative, they are interested in appearances. We have brought the technology associated with work, sports and protective clothing to town wear.' Some of the new materials have presented problems. Oilcloth for instance has been replaced by jersey, which is more flexible. 'At first vinyl used to crack'. In the 1970s 'we bought parachute material for our famous feather nylon raincoats', says Coqueline. 'Our raincoats let air through but they also let in water and our customers are aware of that.' Ever since the synthetic textiles revolution began in the 1960s, Courrèges has been using materials and fibres intended for relatively specialized sectors of the market such as the army, aviation and sport. Believing that clothing would be revolutionized by new materials, he broke down the barriers, the first member of the haute couture fraternity to do so. Other couturiers followed his example in introducing advanced technology into fashion; for instance in 1968 Paco Rabanne and Pierre Cardin experimented with moulded clothes, the 'Giffo' (a raincoat) and the 'Cardine' (a dress).

Unlike them, however, Courrèges combines town wear and sportswear, anticipating present-day trends. As a native of Pau, he has always been interested in rugby and motor racing. His collections reflect his interests; the striped dresses are inspired by the pale-blue and white shirts of the Racing Club de France and the check beachwear by the black-and-white chequered flag used in motor racing. In the 1970s and 1980s Courrèges included various combinations of blousons, raincoats, sweaters,

Bermuda shorts, reefer jackets, trenchcoats, shorts, parkas, down jackets and T-shirts in his ranges. 'Clothes ought to be unconventional. That will be one of the main stylistic trends in both men's and women's clothing.' Like the Italian artist Balla in his 1914 manifesto on futuristic male clothing, Courrèges challenges conventional bourgeois rules. His clothes are beyond fashion, designed to make the wearer feel comfortable. It is certainly an individualistic and contemporary approach.

Since 1965, youth has been the dominant theme in Courrèges' work. Drawing his inspiration from the magical world of childhood, he delays the march of time by 'dressing women in clothes that make them look twenty years younger' (Eugénie Lemoine-Luccioni, *La Robe, suivi d'un entretien avec André Courrèges*, Paris, 1983, p. 155). Chanel was quick to deliver her verdict: 'This man is trying to destroy women by covering up their figures and turning them into little girls' (*Paris-Match*, 1966). A comparison between a 1946 guide to making babies' and children's clothes (Mlle Touzart, *Encyclopédie de la coupe familiale*, volume I, *La Coupe pour enfants*, published in Paris) and the 1960s fashion press is instructive. The encyclopaedia gives patterns for shirts, trousers, capes, shoes (babies' shoes, bootees and shoes with bars), blouses, pinafore dresses with yokes, romper suits and dungarees. The 'childish' style of Courrèges' creations drew comment in the press: *Elle*, for example, mentioned a baby coat (2 March 1967) and an all-in-one shorts outfit (15 February 1971). An illustration in *L'Officiel de la couture* shows a dress with 'bloomers' and a shorts dress (April and September 1967). The Bermuda shorts suit and romper suit are in a similarly youthful style (op. cit., June 1968 and 1969). In February 1972, *Elle* describes Courrèges dresses as 'the kind of dress a little girl would wear for her big sister's wedding'. These descriptions evoke the naïve and innocent world of childhood that lies at the heart of Courrèges' work. The clothes are cut and sewn exactly like children's clothes. A shirt for a little girl is described in the encyclopaedia of 1946 as having 'very wide armholes with the shoulder half-covered'. Many of the dresses Courrèges has designed since 1965 are in that style, inspired by the high plain yokes on little girls' dresses, pinafores and dungarees. In March 1967 *Elle* described 'a real little girl's dress in white wool with pale-blue squares, pleated under a tiny bust and cut away at the shoulders'. The children's clothes have rounded or more usually scalloped edges. 'Scallops replace the hem' in the 1968 collections (*L'Officiel de la couture*, April 1968). Children's kid shoes with straps are worn with socks, also scalloped (*Vogue*, March 1967).

It is clear from the American fashion press, notably *Women's Wear Daily*, that the childhood theme was not the only influence for the radical changes that Courrèges instigated. The flat-heeled boots worn by girl students on campus (5 June 1964), the knitted one-piece jumpsuits for leisure or indoor wear (9 June 1964) and the casual styles favoured by the younger generation in America reflected a new attitude to clothes. In the 1940s Claire

McCardell, Tom Brigance and Tina Leser began applying ideas borrowed from sportswear to the fast-growing ready-to-wear market[2]. Twenty years later, while designers like Michèle Rosier in France were creating completely new ranges of town wear inspired by sportswear, in the traditional world of Paris haute couture Courrèges was a supreme exponent of this modern style, designed for everyday living and not simply for appearances.

Perhaps because of their unconventional approach, André and Coqueline Courrèges have sometimes run into difficulties. Before licences were hastily (and belatedly) introduced in the 1980s, the different couture ranges ('Prototype', 'Couture Future', 'Hyperbole', 'Maille'), perfumes and accessories were under separate management, which was out of step with modern business practice. In the mid-1980s the collections were disrupted for a time when control of the couture and ready-to-wear business was transferred to one such licensee. In autumn 1994 the Courrèges brought out some of their 'trademark' designs again, such as the famous kid boot first seen in 1965. This was widely copied, just as it had been in 1965–67, and as a result they did not hold any more press shows for the next two years. Courrèges then decided to label his creations with the famous AC logo. 'At the beginning we didn't like sending the customers bills. We would send them a little note and two flowers – a daisy from me and a cornflower from André', Coqueline recalls. 'The flowers were intended as a gift. But after three or four years some people said that was naïve. We felt that such criticism was an attack on us. We decided to intertwine our initials like the ones embroidered on linen in old-fashioned trousseaux. Our logo is strongly geometrical. The letters are in circles between the central axis. The initials have to be in the right place, which is different each time. The symbol, the hearts and the famous flowers with the rounded petals that we drew tell love stories.' In unison, of course.

●

In their business affairs, André and Coqueline Courrèges say they are 'creative partners'. André, on being asked in 1970 whether he worked on his own, replied, 'No, I have been working with my wife for the past ten years. She looks after everything. Too much, in fact. I would like her to be more involved in the creative side. I depend on her. I design for women and however much I may try to be intuitive and understanding, inevitably there are times when I feel and react like a man. ... I work very closely with Coqueline.' (*Elle*, 31 August). As if to seal the childlike pact they have entered into in their continual search for new horizons in fashion, design and interior décor, André Courrèges sums it up with the words, 'We see each other just as we are, with no cheating'.

1 All quotations without source references are from the author's conversations with André and Coqueline Courrèges between February and April 1997.

2 See C. Rennolds Millbank, *New York Fashion*, New York, Harry N. Abrams, 1989, and V. Steele, *Women of Fashion*, New York, Rizzoli, 1991.

VOGUE

RIS
OLLECTIONS
RINTEMPS
5

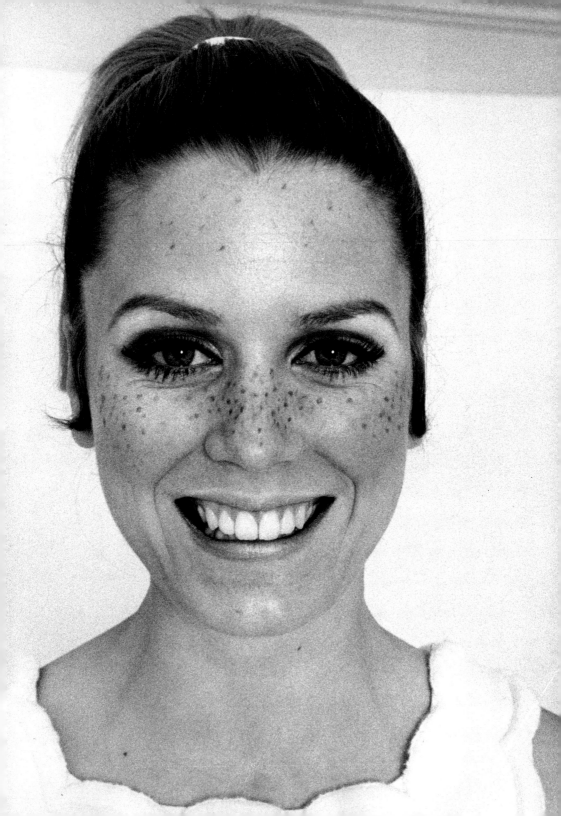

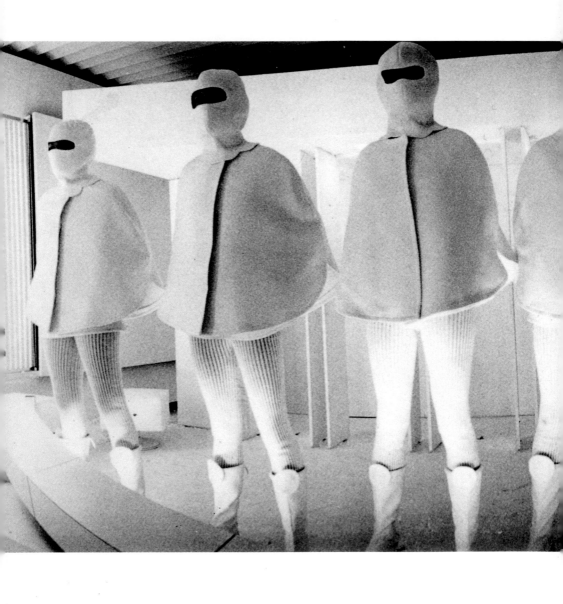

DARK
HORSE
ON A
WHITE
KICK

BAZAAR

Courrèges for
fantasy evenings...

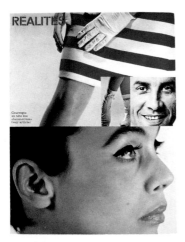

REALITES

VOGUE

THE
LURE
OF
THE
LIFE
AT
HOME

NEW
ENTICEMENTS
IN FASHION,
BEAUTY,
DECORATING

VOGUE'S
CASEBOOK:
3 YOUNG
COUPLES—AND THE
LIFE THAT COUNTS

BEAUTY: THE UPSHOT
OF BARENESS

YOUNG ADVENTURE
IN A CASTLE IN IRELAND

COURRÈGES   ROBES A BRETELLES, JUPES ULTRA-COURTES

Von Fuß bis Kopf
das Neueste,
das Schönste, das
Teuerste, das Billigste
und das Kühnste der
Mode 1970 —
hier fängt es an:
schenkelhohe Stiefel
von Courrèges.
So wie diese Stiefel
aus sehr weichem
Nappaleder
werden die Schuhe
von morgen aussehen:
die Sohle flach
wie bei Turnschuhen,
keine Absätze mehr,
wie eine zweite Haut.
Weg mit den
Schuhen von gestern
und heute.

MIT DIESEN
STIEFELN
IN DIE
ZUKUNFT

Adding a bit of fun to the Courrèges collection — a short, shiny blouse slung casually, teamed with crocheted pants and matching knitted cap, completed with three-foot long needles.

At end of his fun-filled collection in Paris, André Courrèges discusses with Ebony Fashion Fair Producer and Director Mrs. Eunice W. Johnson of the several finest models he featured.

The
French
Whirl
of
Fashion

By Eunice W. Johnson

Ebony
Nov. -74

FROM the runways of Paris to the sidewalks of Harlem, fashion this fall has a new look...

Courrèges' big, hooded sweep vinyl coat to zip-up; pattern is worn over short, orange nylon shirt-dress. Blouse and lacy straight sweater skirt that supported by cross-bodice, a knit hat. Warm up to fall in Courrèges' navy unlined jacket which has vented right-side trim, its worn over a navy body shirt and the new ankle-length, cuffed velvet pants. Completing the costume ensemble: wet boots, of course.

DANIEL
16
PROTO E76

NEW WHEELS
IN TOWN — THE '65 CARS
THE CLOTHES THAT SWITCH THEM ON

At least on the road there was no losing. When the much-balloon-fringed clothes happen, will best cars...

A car that speaks sunshine, convertible good looks: the 1965 Cadillac de Ville convertible comes in a host of hues and wonderful new details, inside & outside. More excitement of new cars and clothes on the next eight pages.

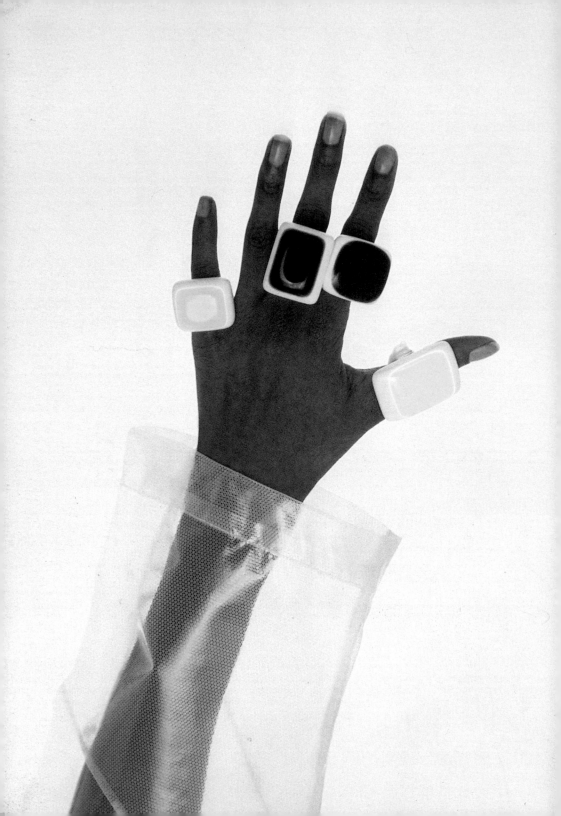

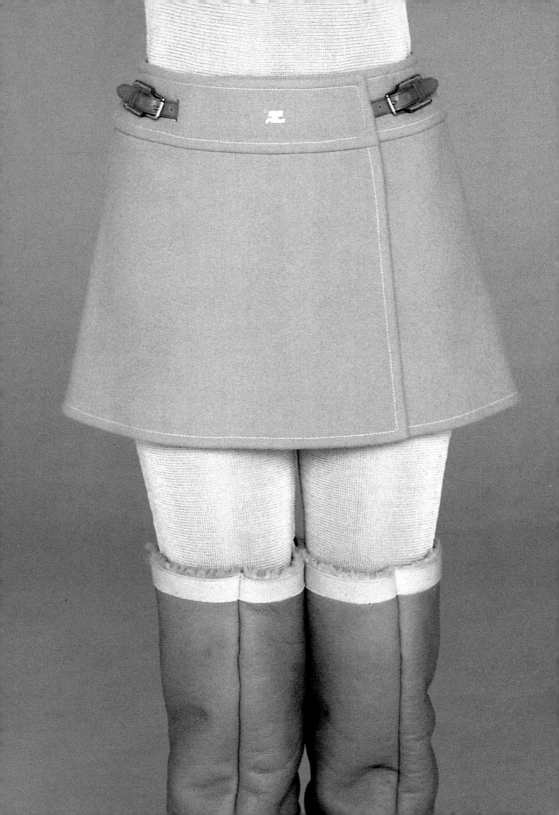

Chronology

1923   March: André Courrèges born in Pau (Pyrénées-Atlantiques). Educated at the National School of Civil Engineering.

1935   July: Coqueline Barrière born in Hendaye (Pyrénées-Atlantiques).

1944   André Courrèges serves as an Air Force pilot based at Aix-en-Provence.

1946   Enrols at the training college for the clothing industries in Paris.

1947   Taken on as a designer at the Jeanne Lafaurie couture house.

1951   André Courrèges starts working for Balenciaga.
Coqueline Barrière, later his 'creative partner', also works there.

1961   In August André and Coqueline Courrèges set up their own Paris couture house. They move into a flat at 48 avenue Kléber, borrowing money from Balenciaga. When they offer to pay him back in 1965, he refuses repayment.

1962   Courrèges shows a collection with 'trousers for day and evening wear'. Designs clothes for Françoise Hardy.

1965   The January collection causes a sensation. Courrèges shows the first ever 'mini'. To finance future expansion Courrèges sells off 50% of the couture house's capital and 100% of the perfume company's capital to L'Oréal. In September he moves to 40 rue François-Ier in Paris. After the Spring/Summer shows in 1965 his designs are widely plagarized and as a result Courrèges does not hold any more press shows until the Spring/Summer shows in 1967. On 2 March 1967, *Elle* refers to these '700 days in retirement' with regret. However he continues to make clothes for his individual customers.

1967   Courrèges launches his haute couture collection 'Couture Future'. Aiming to make couture more accessible, he produces fifteen designs in four or five different sizes, with hemlines to suit the client, and has them mass-produced, enabling them to be sold at a fifth of the usual price.

1968   Because ateliers are becoming hard to find in Paris, Courrèges has a factory built in Pau. On 18 October 1975, *Le Monde* describes the architecture: 'The roof can be opened; it is semi-transparent and the walls are glass. The staff work in contact with nature.'

1969   Designs Romy Schneider's costumes for Claude Sautet's film *Les Choses de la vie*.

1970   Courrèges launches the 'Hyperbole' collection for the mass market. 'Prototype' is the haute couture collection and 'Maille' the knitwear collection. The collections contain a mixture of 'Prototype', 'Couture Future', 'Hyperbole' and 'Maille' designs.

Décor by Courrèges: view of the showroom, rue François-Ier, 1986. © Peter Knapp

First perfume launched, under the name Empreinte.

In the 1960s Courrèges sets up a distribution network of 'exclusive' shops protected against competition. He owns six himself (four in Paris, one in Geneva and one in Munich) and the rest are franchised.

1972 Designs the uniforms for the Munich Olympics.

1973 Designs the 'Courrèges Homme' range for men.

1977 Launches the first fragrance for men, FH77 (Formule Homme 1977).

1979–80 Courrèges introduces a licensing policy.

1982 L'Oréal relinquishes control of the haute couture business and 'Couture Future' and Courrèges transfers it to one of his licensees, the Japanese ready-to-wear firm Itokin, retaining a blocking minority interest.

Sets up 'Courrèges Design' for activities such as property (Perspectives Courrèges development company), cars and food.

1986 After failing to show a collection in 1985, Courrèges loses the Haute Couture label.

1993 Courrèges regains control of the companies and trade marks. Itokin reverts to being a licensee. The Swiss group Burrus buys the perfume business from L'Oréal.

1993–94 Jean-Charles de Castelbajac produces two collections for Courrèges.

1994 Coqueline Courrèges and her team begin reorganizing the management and design structures with, the aim of 'returning to the true Courrèges style'.

1996 Courrèges reacquires the perfume business from the Burrus group.

1997 Launch of the perfume 2020.

André Courrèges exhibits his paintings and sculptures at the FIAC (Foire internationale d'art contemporain) in Paris.

Bibliography

Carter, Ernestine, *Magic Names of Fashion*, London, Weidenfeld & Nicolson, 1980, pp. 130–7.

Lemoine-Luccioni, Eugénie, *Essai psychanalytique sur le vêtement, suivi d'un entretien avec André Courrèges*, Paris, Le Seuil, 1983, pp. 151–61.

Rennolds Milbank, Caroline, *Couture, Les Grands Créateurs*, Paris, Robert Laffont, 1986.

Lobenthal, Joël, *Radical Rags, Fashion of the Sixties*, New York, Abbeville Press, 1990, pp. 40–69.

Special 'Courrèges' issue, *L'Officiel de la couture et de la mode de Paris*, supplement to no. 784, December 1993.

Gervereau, Laurent and Mellor, David (eds.), *Les Sixties, années utopies*, Paris, Somogy, 1996.

White wool trousers with slits, worn over short soft boots. Top-stitched overblouse with dropped shoulders.

© William Klein.

Courrèges

La plage aux clins d'œil, Arman (150 x 130 cm). The collection of glasses is part of the artist's 1986 series 'Hard & soft ware', for which seven symbolic objects were chosen: tailor's scissors, gloves, boots, glasses, socks, caps and bow ties. Photo: Bruno Jarret, © ADAGP, Paris, 1997.
White plastic glasses with slits following the curve of the eyelashes, worn by Mme Filipacchi [Spring/Summer collection 1965]. © Peter Knapp.

Saint-Paul-de-Vence, 1986. Left to right: André Courrèges, Peter Knapp, Arman and Coqueline Courrèges, sitting under the collection of bow ties *Argent qui pleure et Rose qui rit* (130 x 110 cm). The collection of boots entitled *Ne donnez jamais la langue aux chats bottés* (310 x 95 cm; right) is now on a concrete panel in Courrèges' showroom. © Peter Knapp.

Peter Knapp 'satisfies the most urgent, the most childish and indeed the strongest desire aroused by the first miniskirts: to look at legs finally set free and moving under the skirt' (Annie Le Brun, 'A la recherche du temps visible' in *P. Knapp*, Paris Art Center, November 1986). The reversible outfit in double gaberdine opens to reveal a sleeveless top and shorts in Saint-Gall lace. Matching boots (Spring collection 1965). *Elle*, 4 March 1965. © Peter Knapp.

Plain (wool gaberdine) and striped (wool satin) outfits (Spring/Summer collection 1965). Top-stitched seams. White kid open-toed boots with cut-out top. Photo: Willy Rizzo. *Marie Claire*, 1 March 1965. © *Marie Claire*.
The model, starting the show like a motor race, wears an outfit with woven-in sequins on the weft thread (Spring/Summer collection 1965). Photo: Willy Rizzo. *Marie Claire*, 1 March 1965. © *Marie Claire*.

Suit with trousers and blouson jacket, white cotton satin with navy grosgrain braid (Spring/Summer collection 1965). Photo: Willy Rizzo. *Marie Claire*, 1 March 1965. © Marie Claire.
Forneris triple white wool gaberdine coat-dress with navy grosgrain braid. Photo: Willy Rizzo. *Marie Claire*, 1 March 1965. © *Marie Claire*.

Wool-satin dress and jacket with horizontal stripes (Spring/Summer collection 1965). White panama hat. Photo: Willy Rizzo. *Marie Claire*, 1 March 1965. © *Marie Claire*. **Triple wool gaberdine dress** (right: Spring/Summer collection 1965 – see also previous page on right). Plain double wool gaberdine dress and jacket (left: Spring/Summer collection 1967). © The Metropolitan Museum of Art, The Costume Institute, New York.

Trouser suit with sleeveless top in bands of pink and white, woven at the Courrèges atelier, and sequinned pale-green and white dress, woven by Malhia (Spring/Summer collection 1965). Photo taken at the Fondation Maeght, Saint-Paul-de-Vence. © Jeanloup Sieff.
Two-tone dress and jacket (Spring/Summer collection 1967, in preparation. Photo taken at the time the hemline was being adjusted). © Peter Knapp.

At 48 avenue Kléber, 1965. Left to right: Ariane Brener, press officer (seated), Jean-Pierre, manager (standing), André Courrèges (by window), Mme Michel, manager, Marthe, assistant manager, Coqueline Courrèges (sitting in front of them) and Emanuel Ungaro. On the right, two models. © Jeanloup Sieff.
White Panama hat with chinstrap. Cover of Vogue, March 1965. © Helmut Newton/Condé Nast-Vogue Publications.

Many of the outfits in the 1967 Spring/Summer collection feature matching shorts. The much-copied white boots are replaced by flat-heeled shoes. This dress, with a plain yoke and pleated skirt, has matching shorts. Thick socks woven by Courrèges on a mechanical loom. Photo: A. Carrara. Elle, 2 March 1967. © Elle/Scoop. The 'natural' make-up 'bonne mine' (Spring/Summer 1965 collection) was registered as a trademark. © Peter Knapp.

Pastel and white tartan for a wool gaberdine suit (Spring/Summer collection 1968). Courrèges rounded off the cut-outs and revers and even the petals of the hairslides holding the bunches. Photo: Harry Peccinotti. Elle, 29 February 1968. © Elle/Scoop.
First version of the stretch cotton-satin 'bust cover'; cape and shorts suit (around 1968). © Peter Knapp.

'Chiffonnil' by Bianchini-Férier. The flowers are padded with cotton wool on both sides. Detail of a dress in the Victoria and Albert Museum, London (Spring/Summer collection 1967). © Victoria and Albert Museum, London.
After a two-year absence Courrèges shows a new collection (Spring/Summer 1967). The model here is Marisa Berenson. Photo: A. Carrara. © D.R.

From 1966 to 1974 the American photographer Hiro worked exclusively for Harper's Bazaar magazine. This photo session was seen through the lens of his friend Jacques-Henri Lartigue. The models are jumping up and down to make the bells sewn on to their shoe buckles jingle in unison. Hand-knitted socks (Spring/Summer collection 1969). © Ministry of Culture, France/A.A.J.H.L.

Against a soundtrack from a Sergio Leone film the models, in figure-hugging body stockings, stand in an arc. The capes are in a triple fabric – fine cotton on the top and double woollen yarn underneath to create a rounded effect. Dressed in boots and capes, they resemble cosmonauts (Autumn/Winter collection 1968–69). © Peter Knapp.

Two-tone silkscreen-printed mini dress with silver braid (Autumn/Winter collection 1996–97). © Otto Wollenweber.
Pinafore dress in black wool gaberdine with white belt, pockets and buttons, worn over a one-piece white knitted body stocking ('Couture Future' collection 1969-70). © Archives Courrèges.

On the road to Thoiry, 1970. The 'second skin' is a style of clothing that fits the contours of the body exactly. (André Courrèges). © Peter Knapp.
'Second skin' outfit, with blouson jacket and accessories in vinyl (1970). © Peter Knapp.

White acrylic jersey shorts and socks ('Courrèges Maille' collection, Spring/Summer 1971). © Helmut Newton.
'Couture Future' coat, heavy-rib body stocking, garter stitch mittens and cap (1969). © Peter Knapp.

Striped body stocking in garter stitch knit and plain jersey knit (around 1972). It was worn with black vinyl boots. © Peter Knapp.
'Courrèges Maille Hiver' collection 1971–72, with the season's vinyl accessories (cap, glasses and belts with pouches). Photo: Harry Peccinotti. *Elle*, 28 February 1972. © *Elle*/Scoop.

Wool gaberdine coat and dresses (1971). © Peter Knapp.

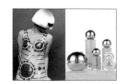

White organza dress embroidered with silver sequins by Jakob Schlaepfer. Brightly coloured nylon wig (Spring/Summer collection 1969). © Peter Knapp.
Empreinte perfume, 1970. © Archives Courrèges.

On the ring road, Porte Maillot, 1968. Zip fronted bolero in check double gaberdine. 'Hipster' trousers. © Peter Knapp.
Courrèges show on the theme of traditional and modern at the temple of Shokoku-ji, Kyoto (1992). The play of light on the aluminium, plastic, vinyl, paper and mirrored clothes is reminiscent of Constructivist (e.g. Rodchenko) design. © Peter Knapp.

The model Gunilia in an organza dress embroidered with silver sequins by Jakob Schlaepfer (Spring/Summer collection 1969). © Peter Knapp.
Two-tone dress woven with sequins (Spring/Summer collection 1965). Photo: Willy Rizzo. *Marie Claire*, March 1965. © *Marie Claire*.

Ski accessories in vinyl and knitted garter stitch (1972). © Peter Knapp.

Golf clubs from 'Sport Futur' collection (1985). © Peter Knapp.
The Munich Olympics, 1972. Centre, white piquet dress designed for students of a rhythmics class; right, white uniform for medics, with shorts and red-braided tunic. The body stocking is the main feature of the uniforms designed for the games. Photo: Denis Reichle. *Elle*, 28 August 1972. © *Elle*/Scoop.

'My sportswear consists of 'practical' clothes like blousons, leotards and bras', Courrèges tells *Vogue* in March 1974 (p. 136–7). © Helmut Newton.

Selection of reports and articles from the British, American, German and French press, 1964 to 1969. © Archives Courrèges.

Plexiglass accessories (Autumn/Winter collection 1997–98). © Otto Wollenweber.
Reversible beige and white miniskirt (Autumn/Winter collection 1996–97). © Otto Wollenweber.

Acknowledgments

The author wishes to thank in particular André and Coqueline Courrèges, Philippe Guillaume, Otto Wollenweber and Peter Knapp, and to acknowledge the assistance and support provided in researching this book by the staff of:
Musée de la Mode de la Ville de Paris, Musé Galliera (Annie Barbéra, Sylvie Roy, Pascal Simon and Catherine Join-Diétterle); the Centre de documentation du Musée de la Mode et du Textile (Emanuelle Montet, Marie-Hélène Poix and Lydia Kamitsis); and the Centre de la documentation de l'IFM (Marie Weigel, Sylvie Dupré and Hélène Kraepiel).
The publisher is grateful to the following for help with illustrations:
Helmut Newton, Bruno Jarret, William Klein and Jeanloup Sieff; thanks are also due to Daniela Ferro (All Rights Reserved), Noémie Mainguet, Gwénaelle Dautricourt (*Marie Claire* Copyright), Claudine Legros (*Elle*/Scoop), Denna Cross (The Metropolitan Museum of Art, New York), Haydn Hansell (Victoria and Albert Museum, London), Martine d'Astier (Association des amis de Jacques-Henri Lartigue), Nicole Chamson (ADAGP, Paris) and Michèle Zaquin (Editions Condé Nast-Vogue)